Life Simplified: Extraordinarily-handy Lifehacks for Ordinary People 2025 Edition

Revised and Updated!

A product of www.LearnedEmpowerment.com

I0116827

LIFE SIMPLIFIED

EXTRAORDINARILY HANDY LIFEHACKS FOR ORDINARY PEOPLE

KENDEL CHRISTENSEN, M.S. ED.

Table of Contents

Thanks for Your Purchase!

I know you will get incredible value out of this resource. **Word-of-mouth is very important for any author to succeed**. Please consider posting a review (http://bit.ly/lifehacksebook) at Amazon and Goodreads.com—even if it is only a few words. Every added review helps. Thanks a lot!

Praise for *Life Simplified:*

"I really love this book. It has so many ideas that are easily implemented (knowing ways to take text out of PDFs and images alone will save me a good bit of time)! I travel fairly often, so the travel hacks are going to make my life easier and more fun. I can't wait to try them all out! But most exciting for me are the hacks that protect my security and privacy online."

- Tom Arnold, Software Training Specialist (Durham, NC)

"These tips are a must. With one of the entertainment 'lifehacks', I now have absolute control of the content I choose to watch on my living room T.V. The variety and quality are fantastic. Being recently retired from a busy, stressful career, I refuse to spend my time on things of little worth. Life is too short. I have yet to try out lots of these ideas but WOW, the ones I have tried, I LOVE! His section on learning hacks gave me a way to read outstanding books I never would have thought I had time for. The Food, Fitness, and Travel sections have saved me time in the kitchen, given me fitness tips that I now use every day, and have saved me time and money on an upcoming trip to Florida. This book is worth its weight in gold. So glad I found

it!"
- Janet, Retired special education teacher, grandmother, charter school board chair (Salt Lake City, UT)

"These ideas are life-saving. I'm a young professional in a busy metropolitan city so time is precious to me. Having a book full of reliable, helpful, and time-saving tips has been amazing. I am not tech savvy at all, so having a reference where I am able to look at see if what I'm trying to accomplish can be done more efficiently has been helpful on many occasions. I also loved the section on food. Because the cooking tips were so helpful and easy, it has made me rethink stopping for takeout on the way home from work more than once! Before reading this book I knew that there were finance websites out there, but I didn't know which were trustworthy, or easiest to work with. After reading the book I was able to set up an account with one of the sites and easily create a budget that makes sense for me, and in turn increase the amount of money I am saving monthly."
- Emilee Thomas, Physician Assistant (New York, NY)

"Life seems more complex than ever, with ever-multiplying demands on our attention and deadlines that feel like they come more rapidly all the time. It also feels like the modern world is filled with people who are ingenious and dedicated in their goal of taking our money. This book is filled with helpful tips that help reduce complexity and save money, and therefore help deal with these two problems. I was amazed to find out how many websites, apps, and resources had already been created to help with many of the (productive and non-productive) things I already do – budgeting, time management, watching movies, traveling, and working with technology. Without this book, I would never have known about this wealth of resources. Life will be a little less complex and a little more affordable after reading this book."

- Bradford Tuckfield, PhD candidate, Wharton School of Business (Philadelphia, PA)

Welcome

Hi, my name is Kendel Christensen, founder of LearnedEmpowerment.com. I'm a lifelong learner and collector of all things worthy of the distinction "life-changing." I wrote this book for two main reasons:

1. I believe a few smart ideas—effectively applied and taken together—can add up to make a *huge* difference over time in the results one gets out of life. There has been a wealth of time, energy, and money-saving advances in technology and human knowledge that can exponentially impact your personal enjoyment, productivity, and unique contribution to the world. If you can find those "better ways" to simplify some areas of your life, you'll get better results in all areas.

2. I wanted to organize the best "quick win" tips I've accumulated over the years into a handy resource to benefit others. I've referred to this list on a daily basis and want to give you the same advantages I've gained by utilizing these tools and tips.

You may have heard the term "lifehack" (also "life

hack") before: perhaps a friend shared one on Facebook, or you've watched some YouTube videos that boast the greatest or newest or most essential lifehacks that you need to know. If you haven't, a lifehack is simply a procedure that (often creatively) solves or reduces the difficulty of common problems in life. Such as putting a cutting board over an open kitchen drawer to get a bit more counter space, or using binder clips to keep power cords organized.

I've gone through innumerable lifehack lists on blogs and scoured the "best lifehacks ever" video compilations. Some hacks are truly amazing, others are trivial, and still others don't work at all. This book is a summary of the best hacks I've found that will enable you to do more things, better. I hope you save as much time and energy as I have by using them.

If there is an amazing hack you've personally tried that has made a significant difference in the quality of your life, I'd love to hear about it.

Happy hacking!

- Kendel Christensen
www.LearnedEmpowerment.com

Special Offer

Thank you for investing in yourself! I sincerely hope the time you invest in this book will pay off 10 fold. As a special thank you for getting this book, I want to give you a **free gift** that has helped me **beat procrastination** and **stay motivated**.

I'll give you access to a collection of quotations, put on beautiful backgrounds, that instantly put me in a forward-thinking, energetic state of mind. I refer to them every time I don't feel like working, and they inspire me without fail.

Here is the link to this free gift:
Learnedempowerment.com/LifeSimplified-gift
Thanks again.

Committed to your success,
-Kendel

How to Use This Book

Life Simplified is divided into 16 categories of lifehacks. I've tried to make each tip as short and digestible as possible – just go to a category that interests you, and in a matter of minutes you'll have amazing ideas to immediately take advantage of.

I use a "star" (★) system to rank each lifehack within its category. **The more ★'s, the more useful or widely applicable the tip is (in my subjective opinion).**

If you are not very familiar with computers and the internet, the following resources may be overwhelming. Even the hacks that sound amazing will still take a bit of investigating to integrate into your life. I recommend starting with the category that most interests you; try **one** hack in that category per week (or month) to get the most out of this book.

I have include many links (identified by blue text) in this book. If you are reading this on an internet-browser-enabled device, tapping on the link will take you to that website. For those who do not have ready internet access, I have included shortlinks in parentheses (Amzn.to/1yYZGQv) which can be easily input into a browser or other internet-enabled device. The links are valid as of January, 2025.

Also, you can visit the respective app store (e.g. Google Play or the Apple App Store) to find any mobile device apps that I mention in relation to a recommended website.

And now... to the lifehacks!

Entertainment Lifehacks

Movies & TV

★★★★ Free movies and TV shows

Get free (ad-supported) movies *and* Tv Shows through Tubi (https://tubitv.com/) and Pluto.tv Just visit the site (or download their apps) and check out their content. No registration required.

Kanopy.com has a wide selection if your local library supports it.

—Bonus tip: I recommend you check out this excellent article (https://www.lifewire.com/watch-free-movies-online-1356647) by Stacy Fisher that keeps up to date info about the best free online movie services. SO great.

18 Best Places to Watch Free Movies Online
Watch Movies Online for Free

By Stacy Fisher
Freebies Expert

Updated March 02, 2018

Sign Up for Our
Free Newsletters

Watching free movies online is a convenient and frugal way to see the movies you love right from the comfort of your own home. All you'll need to watch these free online movies are a computer or TV with an Internet connection.

More useful content streaming sites:

- To stream videos with content filters, check out VidAngel.com
- For a search engine that keeps tabs on where

you can stream any movie online, try
JustWatch.com. It will tell you which services
carry which movies and shows at what prices.
Yidio.com and PlayPilot.com are both good
alternatives.

- PBS.org/explore streams many (though not
  all) PBS for free, including almost 2-dozen of
  the popular NOVA series (with ads).

★★★★ Movie suggestion sites

Having trouble finding something to watch? Here are
some great tips:

- Type the word "movies" and [your zipcode]
  (e.g., "movies 22202" without the quotes) into
  Google and the popular movies playing in
  your area will appear in your search results.
  Just click on the cover art for the movie, and
  Google will display the rating, running time,
  IMDB/Rotten Tomatoes/MetaCritic rating,
  even a link to the trailer—all at a glance!

- InstantWatcher.com ranks what is currently on
  popular streaming services by critical acclaim
  (as established by IMDB, Rotten Tomatoes
  and/or MetaCritic).

- aGoodMovieToWatch.com Suggests GREAT
  lesser-known movies based off your mood and
  types you like.

- Like scary movies… but only a *certain kind* of

scary? Find the right balance among gore, suspense, and "disturbing" at ReelScary.com.

Internet Videos & Games

★★★★ Watch enlightening content for less
Made by the founder of the Discovery Channel, Curiositystream.com is your gateway to more enlightening video content. Though it has cut ties with the Nebula streaming service (basically all the best edutainment YouTubers' videos are there, ad-free), When I did get both those services bundled, I completely replaced YouTube premium, saving myself over $100/yr.

★★★★ Sometimes, you're just in the mood for a puzzle!
Jigsawexplorer.com is a great find if you want to relax putting together a "just right" puzzle to occupy 20 minutes at a time. BONUS: You can invite a friend (or long distance dating partner) to do the puzzle in real time together, remotely! I've done this oodles and it pleases *every time.*

★★★ Watch Broadway Shows Online

BroadwayHD.com has a selection of broadway productions to stream online for a small fee. Great option for a way to watch the theatre without actually having to go there!

★★★ Old arcade games at Archive.org

How does an internet archive of tons of old, classic arcade games sound? The games play in your browser and they actually work! I even found treasures like Q-bert & Street Fighter II—classic. Archive.org/details/internetarcade. They also recently added Windows 3.1 games. Ski Free forever! If you look in the film archive, there's a lot there as well. Be aware, though, as some of the material is adult-themed.

The Software Library screenshot showing collection of software titles including MS-DOS, Windows 3.x, Apple Computer, Prince of Persia, Pac-Man, SimCity, and others with 43,787 items.

★★★ YouTube hacks

- I can't believe more people don't use this (Dramatically improves watch rates for links you make if… you know, you want them to actually watch what you send them). Add "&t=[time]H:[time]M:[time]S" (replace [time] with how many hours, minutes and seconds). For example, if you want the video to start at hour, 41 minutes and 0 seconds, the URL would look like https://youtu.be/VIDEO_ID**&t=1h41m20s**
- I just learned the keyboard shortcuts to skip

ahead in a video (press l on the keyboard) and go backwards 10 seconds at a time (the j key).

- SafeShare.tv enables you to share YouTube videos on a clean, gray background. The site strips all the extra clutter like comments and related videos (no more embarrassing "watch next" suggestions!).

★★★ More entertaining time-killers

If you don't have enough ways to distract yourself yet, StumbleUpon.com is completely addictive. You basically fill in your interests, click "stumble" and the site shows you highly-rated sites liked by people who selected the same interests as you. A few other especially effective timewasters I've found are Clickhole.com and Pleated-jeans.com and BoredPanda.com. Don't say I didn't warn you!

Email Lifehacks

★★★★★ Dead simple email reminders

Have FollowUpThen.com send you free reminder

emails, when you need them. Send an email reminder that will "come back" to your inbox (e.g., 3weeks@followupthen.com), or... Ever send an email get forgotten when the other person forgets to get back to you? Help yourself out by selecting a number of days that you'd like to be reminded to follow up with the person (e.g., 5), and include the following email address on the **bcc** (blind carbon copy) line: 5days@followupthen.com. Like magic, you (only) will be sent a reminder email in 5 days—just enough time to follow up before the deadline makes it an emergency. If you add a followupthen address to the **cc** (carbon copy) line, the site will send the reminder to **both** of you.

—Followup.cc offers similar features (though a paid service).

★★★★★ Spam reducers

Addy.io creates a temporary e-mail for you to use when signing up for websites and services to reduce spam in your primary email account.

10MinuteMail.com is a great alternative (also free). I use it every time I sign up for a questionable offer or an unproven service. Fewer emails to sort through = More time available.

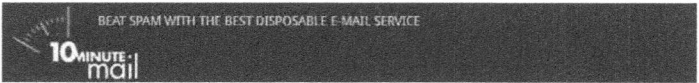

BEAT SPAM WITH THE BEST DISPOSABLE E-MAIL SERVICE

10MINUTE·
mail

Welcome to 10 Minute Mail! This is your temporary mail address:

c1328410@mvrht.com **0 7 : 5 1**

YOU HAVE 1 MESSAGE(S).

▸ automated@   Please confirm your e-mail address ·

★★★★★ Subscription management

Unroll.me is amazing. You can unsubscribe in bulk from all the lists you've signed up for over time and then consolidate the subscriptions you want to keep into ONE daily email. I unsubscribed from 196 unwanted subscriptions in 8 minutes flat— plus it's life-changing *and* free!

★★★★ Supercharge your single Gmail address do the work of multiple addresses

So you have a shiny "youremail@gmail.com" and you use it for everything. Did you know that that one Gmail address actually has multiple extra ones built-in? It's true! You can do this in a few ways:

1. Add "+[word]" (without brackets) at the end of your Gmail address but before the @ symbol. For example, any email sent to "youremail+decoy1@gmail.com" still arrives at "youremail@gmail.com"'s inbox.

2. You can also modify your Gmail address with periods: your.name@gmail.com is the <u>same</u> as y.ourname@gmail.com and yourname@gmail.com (meaning any email sent to those addresses will all arrive to the same place).

3. Finally, you can change @gmail to @googlemail.com, and you will still receive emails sent to either address.

Why is this SO GREAT? A few reasons:

- You can sign up for MULTIPLE promotional offers with the SAME email address. More "free trials" here I come! ("youremail+decoy1@gmail.com" is treated *as if* it were youremail@gmail.com—but the service you signed up for doesn't know that!)

- You can filter emails easier. If you're signing up for a website that you think will send you unwanted ads, you can modify your email address to include the filter keyword "offers"—"johndoe**+offers**@gmail.com."

Create an "Offers" folder in your Gmail account, and set up a filter to move all incoming messages sent to johndoe**+offers**@gmail.com to that folder. Dating sites are another great example; sign up using "youremail+datingsite@gmail.com," create a "Dating" folder, and setup a Gmail filter to send all the emails coming to that address to your Dating folder. Credit to Jillian D'Onfro's article from Business Insider: (Businessinsider.com/awesome-google-features-you-didnt-know-existed-2014-7?op=1)

- Again, the basic point is ONE email address for MULTIPLE purposes; you could use your.name@gmail.com for friends, yourname@gmail.com for work, and your.name@googlemail.com for websites or specific projects. If you want to find emails from just your friends, you would search your inbox for messages sent to your.name@gmail.com; to track that specific project, you would search for your.name@googlemail.com, etc. Stop having to log in to 20 different email inboxes today!

★★★★ Email delivery management

Perhaps the biggest drain on productivity is constant

distraction. Email is often the biggest culprit. Minimize distractions by receiving emails when *you* choose with BatchedInbox.com.

Settings:

○ Deliver emails:

⦿ twice ▾ daily at 9am ▾ and 12am (midnight) ▾

| 12am (midnight) |
| 1am |
| 2am |
| 3am |
| 4am |
| 5am |
| 6am |
| 7am |
| 8am |
| 9am |
| 10am |
| 11am |
| 12pm (noon) |
| 1pm |

◌ every hour on the hour

◉ Your timezone:

America/New_York ▾

Next

need help or have any questions or suggestions? er, or give back

Though now built in to most email clients worth their salt, Another tool you can use to "pause" email is a service called boomerang, just go to InboxPause.com.

Google

Gmail ▾ PAUSE

COMPOSE

Family & Children Lifehacks

★★★★ Bring your kids FOR FREE
The *fantastic* Freebie Guy (thefreebieguy.com) have compiled a list of places where kids get in and/or eat for free. Definitely worth checking out.

★★★★ Free online games for children
Britt Lynn over at www.bestkidstuff.com has a list of the best free online games and videos for kids.
https://www.bestkidstuff.com/entertainment/best-free-online-games-for-kids/
BONUS: For even more of an education focus list, (National Geographic and ABCya being standouts), definitely check out
https://www.prodigygame.com/main-en/blog/free-games-for-kids/
RELATED: SuperSimpleLearning.com makes hyper engaging educational videos for littler kids. Very useful.

★★★ Movie rating guides
As I do not trust movie and TV ratings nowadays, I check out KidsInMind.com, IMDB.com's parents

guide (found on a movie's specific site), and/or CommonSenseMedia.org to get an idea of what exactly is in a movie beforehand.

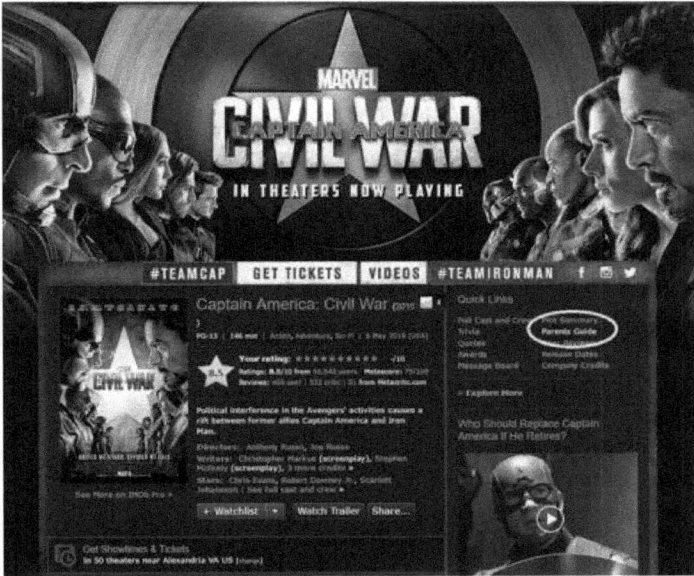

★★★ Family friendly internet filtering

https://www.opendns.com/setupguide/#familyshield is the simplest free way I have found to put a family-friendly filter on your internet.

★★★ Enjoy Children's Books Read Aloud in the Best Voices

There's a website dedicated to bringing books alive by big celebrities reading children's books for free.

https://storylineonline.net Check it out!

★★★ Oww! not allowed:

Kids… get cut and fall down. One of THE BEST pro tips I've gotten from the parenting support groups I'm a part of is: keep a band-aid or 2 in your wallet (or purse). I use 'em *all the time.*

★★★ Autographed Disney pictures

If you send a handwritten letter to Disney, they will send you an autographed postcard or picture of your favorite Disney character! The picture will arrive with 4-6 weeks. Here are the addresses:

Attn: [Favorite Disney Character]
Walt Disney World Communications
P.O. Box 10040
Lake Buena Vista, FL 32830-0040

Walt Disney Company
Attn: Fan Mail Department
500 South Buena Vista Street
Burbank, CA 91521

The picture should arrive with 4-6 weeks.
(Credit to Kristin from Couponing to Disney (Bit.ly/1xAzxJO).

★★ Keep an online eye on your kids

Want to keep an eye on your little ones remotely?

Install a remote monitoring app like <u>Presence</u> (<u>Bit.ly/176tFQ1</u>) for your smart device (e.g., Android or iPhone/iPad) and watch them online from where you're working.

★★ No more monkeys falling off the bed
Scared of your kids falling out of bed? Put a pool noodle *under the fitted sheet…* problem solved!

Food Lifehacks

★★★★★ **Get hundreds of dollars of free or discounted meals sent to your door.**

We live in a golden age of convenience. You may know about a few meals kit-to-your-door services. But do you know how to hack each one to get the maximum benefit? Deals change over time, but at the time of writing, <u>here is a great place to get dozens of free or discounted meals</u> (or just Google "how to get the best meal kit deals) with fresher, higher quality ingredients than what cooking for yourself usually entails. I've gotten hundreds of dollars worth of food for basically free!

★★★★ **Never peel a potato, deal with pomegranate seeds, or shuck corn again**

Never peel another potato again. Score the potato at the midway point, boil the potato with the skin on for ~10 minutes, then put into icy-cold water for five seconds and rotate the peel off with your hands going in different directions. Bam. Done. Watch this video to see this method in action: <u>Youtu.be/z4W0qIPJmoo?t=27s</u>. This method works with the skin of many fruits and veggies too! Also, when making mashed potatoes (my favorite) use Russet/baker potatoes for maximum "fluff"—so good! Red potatoes are also good but these suggestions are based, of course, on preference.

—De-seed a pomegranate in 10 seconds using a three-step method: Cut the pomegranate in half. Gently pull the sides apart. Take one of the halves and hit it **hard** on the peeling with a wooden spoon while you rotate it. See the method in action at Youtu.be/O6jyOqiFbBM (Credit: NaturalMarketer).

—Another food hack worth mentioning is avoiding the silky mess from shucking corn. Simply microwave the corn for ~5minutes, cut about one inch off the bottom (where the round stem is), then shake it out while holding it from the top (while wearing oven mitts). Credit to VACH from Instructables: Instructables.com/id/How-to-never-shuck-corn-again. Note: this method does slightly affect the flavor of the corn.

★★★★ Keep baked goods fresh

Want to keep that "from-the-oven" moistness of cookies longer? Store the cookies in an air-tight container with a small slice of an apple (or white bread). It works!

★★★ Make bacon even better (it's possible!)

Bake bacon in the oven rather than in a frying pan. Eliminate uneven sides, crumbly middles, hard ends—even lessen shrinkage! Preheat oven to 400°, lay the bacon strips flat on a baking sheet with sides high enough to catch the grease, and bake ~12-17 minutes. Also, if you slightly crinkle tin foil and line the baking sheet, you'll catch a lot of the bacon grease and make clean up easier (the foil also helps keep the bacon from sticking to the pan). Credit to Trish from MomOnTimeout.com (Bit.ly/1C3nQAL) and Tom Arnold for the clean-up tip!

★★ Soften cold butter quickly

Soften a portion of that too-hard-because-it-has-been-in-the-fridge butter by putting a warm glass over it (Youtu.be/SWGBLkdm5h0).

★★ Keep bananas fresh, longer

Potassium is a good thing for your body. Bananas are

its packaging. Make your good, potassium-filled bananas last longer for you by wrapping the top stems in plastic wrap. It's a real thing.

★ Fresh egg check
When put in water, fresh eggs *sink* while stale eggs *float*.

Other useful lifehack websites for food
- SuperCook.com enables you to enter the ingredients you have available and it will give you meal ideas from what you already have.
- MyFitnessPal.com (Bit.ly/176uf0c) lists all the ingredients of your recipe, and it will calculate the calories of your final product for you. Currently free!

Household Lifehacks

★★★★★ **Make money from your old junk**

Sell your stuff on Facebook Marketplace or local classifieds. Sounds obvious, true, but I know SO MANY people that don't think about or do this! Think of your entire life and how many things you just donated (or just threw away). Think of having $$ in your pocket again instead! Just take a picture, write a short description, and post it (Don't post just anything, but over time you will get a sense of what will sell quickly or not—my rule of thumb is 30% lower than retail price). I have made over $30,000 over the course of my life for doing this (Bonus hack: I force myself to downsize 1/3 of my possessions every time I move—highly recommended as well!)

★★★★★ **Stop Fighting Your Shower**

This saves me and every single one of my guests time, every day. Put white out or nail polish at the EXACT spot your shower valve needs to be to have a decent temperature. Seconds saved, every day.

★★★★★ Opt out of junk mail

I detest junk mail and most anything else I have to process unnecessarily. CatalogChoice.org opts you out of lists of junk mail being sent to your house—for free! Bliss! Also, when a telemarketer calls, hanging up lets them re-use your number in the system later. Instead, **specifically ask** to *not be called again*. They are required by law to flag your number as off limits.

★★★★★ Command hooks

Read this article (https://lifehacker.com/15-brilliant-things-you-can-do-with-command-hooks-1355369802) on the many uses of Command hooks around the house. Like right now. I audibly gasped with delight a half dozen times. Stand-out entries include: putting a hook upside down on your trash bins and pulling the bag over it such that it 'grabs' the bag; using them to organize your pot lids on the inside cupboard door (two on the bottom at about the

5 and 8 o'clock positions); and mounting toothbrushes or tablet computers! *This is also a good read on the same subject: Bit.ly/buzzhooks.*

★★★★ Clean dishes the least-icky way
Hear me out on this one: I detest the feel of scrubbing

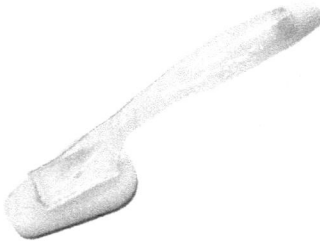

dirty dishes. Enter:

It's not JUST a handle that keeps me from having to get my hands all nasty (and get a better angle), oh no. It's also a reservoir of dish soap so it saves you time and energy there too! Primitive, but sooooo effective!

★★★★Speaking of sinks, Use a Tension Rod Under Your Sink:
Hanging bottles above and baskets below (I use old amazon boxes) means a refreshingly ordered kitchen.

Credit: 17apart.com

★★★★ Save money on your water bill with this toilet trick

Want to put potentially hundreds of dollars back in your pocket EVERY YEAR? Simply fill up a 1-liter bottle with water (and a few small rocks to keep it submerged) and put it in your toilet tank. It will still flush, but the water savings are significant over time!

★★★ Eliminate fruit flies and ants

Get rid of pesky fruit flies by simply putting some fruit in a dish, covering it with plastic wrap, and poking a small hole at the top. Easy to get in, almost

impossible to get out! Credit to Grant Thompson, the King of Random (<u>Bit.ly/1ya5yM8</u>). I love this!
—Ant problems? Spread cornmeal or coffee grounds around their territory. They'll leave after a few days.

★★★ Three laundry hacks

Ironing is too much work! Spraying your clothes lightly with water and hanging them to dry (~30 minutes), though it takes a tad longer, is definitely easier for those who prefer not to spend time slaving over clothes with a hot iron. Some say that putting items in the dryer (just 5-10 minutes) with some ice cubes also works wonders. Want a cheap, reusable alternative to dryer sheets? Try crumpling up balls of aluminum foil to get rid of static cling. It works! (The downsides being it doesn't soften the clothes and makes the dry cycle slightly louder.)

★★★ Maximize space in your house

House too small? Be creative with every inch of your space: put over-the-door shoe holders on doors (e.g., pantry door for food items, cleaning products for the closet door, electronic gadgets or office supplies for the study), get bed risers and take advantage of storage space under your bed, use tension rods to make extra closet or storage space (e.g., hang all your cleaning supplies under the sink, or make an extra shelf in a cupboard).

★★★ Open Hard-to-open jars

Vexed with a jar lid that won't budge? Try wrapping a
rubber band (the "thicker" type is better) around it a
few times. Presto! You now have a better grip, and
now have a better chance of getting the lid off. If you
don't have any thick rubber bands, multiple thin ones
also can work, just slightly less effectively.

BONUS rubber band tip: Wrap them around the ends
of clothes hangars to help prevent your clothes from
falling off as much.

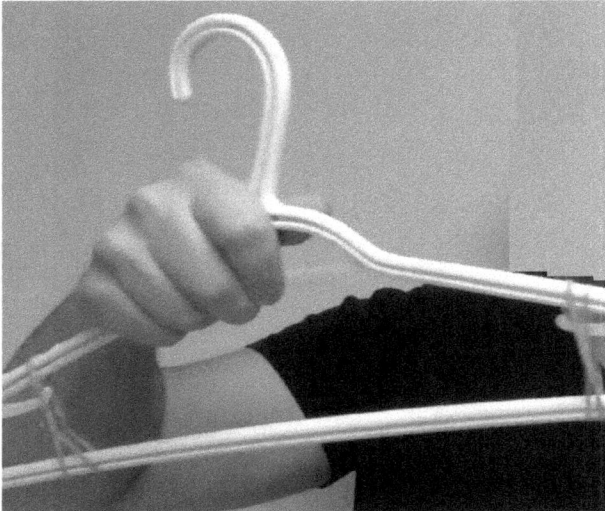

★★ Dry clothes faster

Dry clothes a bit faster by putting the wet clothes in with a dry towel—the catch is you have to take the towel out of the dryer after about ~15 minutes, otherwise it contributes to the overall moisture. Credit to Dylan of Household Hacker.

★★ Go paperless

Reduce clutter by throwing away all the old papers you have lying around. Still having a hard time saying goodbye to something you might want to refer to later? Scan it into your computer or take a picture of it before recycling.

Knowledge-enhancing Lifehacks

★★★★★ **Multitask with educational videos**
Become one of the most educated people around: install an old tablet or cheap Chromebook at a place where you regularly clean or prep (e.g., the kitchen) to watch educational videos while you work (the key is keeping the device plugged in and on so that you can press play easily).

Get some of the best educational videos at Ted.com, and view this document (Bit.ly/1rLdi4v) which ranks them by level of engagement (for a more up-to-date list of the most life-changing talks, check out LearnedEmpowerment.com/my-personal-favorite-ted-talks).

Also, many authors give excellent insights from their books when they present at Google—and Google posts their talks for *free* at Youtube.com/user/AtGoogleTalks or just, you know plug in to over 1,700 free online university courses from the likes of Yale, Oxford, MIT, and Harvard.

★★★★★ **Lifelong Learning, SUPER-charged**
Sure, the "university of youtube" is your go-to

resource to teach you all things under the sun (I've saved thousands by learning how to fix all sorts of things myself) as well as upped all my professional credentials. But if you want to "level up" your learning, I've gotten oodles of value through sites like www.Udemy.com TheGreatCoursesPlus.com and LinkedIn Learning They cost money (Udemy has DEEP sales often!) but LinkedIn at the time of this writing has relationships where you can get access free through your local library. Take courses on things that interest you, improve yourself and social skills, and perhaps best of all, zero in on really specific skills where experts go into great depth, much more than free alternatives.

Love free audiobooks? Libby (LibbyApp.com) has almost as many audiobooks as $15/mo Audible, including new releases, for FREE through most local libraries (also Hoopla HooplaDigital.com).

--Of specific note, Coursera has "The Science of Well-being" and "The ABC's of Children" by Alan Kazdin for FREE and they have ABSOLUTELY changed my life (for everyone, the latter if you truly NEVER are around kids, fine. But even if you're not a parent and only occasionally interact with kids it's a MUST!)

★★★★★ De-Toxify Where You Get Your News

It's a personal mission of mine to help heal the political divide in America, and a necessary step in that is breaking free of biased and one-sided news sources that can give a slanted side and paints the *other* side as one-dimensional "villains."

Enter Allsides.com TheFlipSide.io NewsAsFacts.com and Ground.news Each has a different approach, but each goes out of its way to remove bias and show a more objective presentation of the facts, or at least tell you which way news reporting slants and why.

Be a patriot: Be informed, but not with sources that have an agenda or want to trigger you.

★★★★★ Easy reading

Don't have time to read a popular (nonfiction) book? Try checking SlideShare.net or Googling "filetype:ppt (or pptx) [name of book]" (without brackets and quotes)—you'll often find amazing presentations that summarize the concepts brilliantly! I use this all the time. A **great** service that summarizes books for you for a monthly fee is Blinkist.com

★★★★★ Kindle highlights

Did you know that anything you highlight on your Amazon Kindle device or app gets transcribed for you into a personal highlights database? It's true! Check out Kindle.Amazon.com/your_highlights. You can copy and paste your highlights into documents or (my recommendation, Evernote).

★★★★★ Virtual bookshelf with Goodreads.com

If you love books at all, join Goodreads.com right now and friend me. Goodreads keeps a virtual bookshelf of all the books you have read, prompts you to make progress on the books you are reading (the site has kindle integration), but 2nd best of all: it's social. You can see what your friends are reading (and comment on their progress), and give and receive recommendations. The service itself will also give you recommendations based off of books you have previously enjoyed.

BEST of all: You don't have to read a book before book club! Well, you still should. But, in a pinch: go to the "quotations" section and popular books will have *all* the most highlighted quotes listed in order. You get a certified "best of" the book, crowd-sourced from tens of millions of kindle readers. BAM.

★★★★ Send annotated websites

Add comments and highlights to websites, then send friends the personalized, annotated version of the website with Diigo.com

★★★★ Online flash cards

Put information into your long-term memory with the Anki (Apps.ankiweb.net) flashcard app; the site uses an algorithm to calculate the optimal time to show a card again. Widely used to learn languages, or studying for tests. In fact, users can share their flashcard creations with the community for FREE. If you are studying a language or a common college course, chances are, someone has made a sweet deck for you already! Studying on the go? There are apps that sync with your mobile devices!

Intelligent.
Powerful.
Friendly.
FREE.

Introducing **Anki**, the spaced repetition software (SRS) flashcard program designed to make you the smartest person you can be.

★★★★ **Test out of expensive college classes**

Save enormous amounts of time and money on college by testing out of some 33 commonly-required college classes in 5 subject areas using CLEP (Clep.CollegeBoard.org). CLEP tests give you credit in almost 3000 colleges and universities. Think of the tuition money an $80 test could save you! Also consider Elearners.com/online-certificate-programs to get alternative certifications and credentials.

★★★★ **Be Informed on the Toughest Issues**

Intelligence Squared is currently my favorite podcast (http://www.intelligencesquared.com/podcast). They ask the most provocative/controversial issues of our day (e.g., "Is technology making us dumber?" or "Does China do capitalism better than America?"), then get the leading experts **on both sides** to give their **best arguments**, and the audience votes for which side convinced them the most.

Tickets are $40 to each event… but they post the FULL videos on their website for FREE! Check them out at: https://opentodebate.org/debates/#

Oh, and did I mention they also post how the audience voted before and after the debate, as well as the research from each panelist?

To get personally involved in more-productive-than-social-media debates, I recommend Kialo.com which has a variety of topics and questions which you can make claims about and comment on other people's claims (then see how many people vote for your claims)

★★★★ Make Better Decisions

Nobel prize-winning researcher Daniel Kahneman gave me an idea that has CHANGED MY LIFE: Before you make a decision, imagine its in the future and the idea/project has failed. Really force yourself to examine why it did. Kahneman claims (and I agree) it makes implementing the idea (or rejecting it) *significantly* better.

★★★ Regain knowledge forgotten from high school

Refresh everything you should (or could) have learned in school in an entertaining way by checking out the CrashCourse (Bit.ly/186Khr3) YouTube channel!

★★★ Learn almost anything for free

The internet gives access to more free things. Check out this list of how to learn many worthwhile things for free—from programming to cooking to languages at NoExcuseList.com. You should also know about Project Gutenberg, a collection of tens of thousands of books in the public domain (Gutenberg.org). Alternatively, you can download a nifty free books app for iOS called Ultimate Classics Library https://itunes.apple.com/us/app/free-books-ultimate-classics/id364612911?mt=8

★★★ Save online articles for later

Pocket (GetPocket.com) is a simple, cross-platform app/extension that lets you save any online article to read later when you're offline (or just in a different location—I save articles on my computer, then read them on my phone when I am waiting in line, riding transit, etc.).

★★★ Book read time estimated for you

HowLongToReadThis.com Has the average reading times for all the most popular books. It can even generate a personalized reading speed based on an excerpt from the book. Supa' coo'. *Amazon Kindle offers a similar service (when reading a book on their*

Kindle platform).

★★ Generate interactive timelines
Create an interactive timeline with (in order of preference), Preceden.com, Tiki-toki.com, Similewidgets.org.

★★ Upgrade your research
For anyone who does research, check out Zotero.org and Endnote.com to keep better track of all the sources you cite.

★★ Is this BS or credible?
PolitiFact (Politifact.com) won a Pulitzer Prize for fact-checking for a reason. Check it out before you share something. FactCheck.org (Factcheck.org)has likewise been found to be extremely reliable and Snopes.com will tell you if a story or offer of dubious origin (such as a mass email) is real or a scam.

★★ Word clouds
Wordle.net creates beautiful word clouds from text to help the main ideas surface. Also great for creating word clouds as gifts for friends, or generating artistic typographic art on topics that are important to you.

★★ Rhyme dictionary

RhymeZone.com is a rhyme dictionary. Type in a word and get a list of rhyming and near-rhyming words! This is a game-changer if you want to write a poem or song, or when you want to express something in a clever way.

★★ Etymologies

EtymOnline.com gives you the history behind any word.

Money-saving Lifehacks

★ ★ ★ ★ ★ Money management

Use CreditKarma.com or Rocket Money ($) to manage your money. Really, I can't tell you how convenient having all of your account transactions in one place is—I know exactly how my net worth changes every day! In addition, similar sites lets you set finance goals, and nudges you to make smarter choices with your money. They even enable you to receive free credit scores!

--Also, I'm not a financial adviser, but talk to one about getting a ROTH IRA. In my opinion, THE BEST Wealth-generating decision a person can often make!

★ ★ ★ ★ ★ Get *Amazon.com* products at steep discounts or FREE

Sites like Snagshout.com and MyVipon.comhttps://www.amzreviewtrader.com/ are havens for deal hunters. All you have to do is promise to write a review for the products, and BAM! You get access to discount codes on awesome, quality products. I've bought over 100 items and can't recommend it highly enough (be honest in your posts!).

★★★★★ **Get stuff for free because it is your birthday**

Ever wanted a comprehensive list of all the places that give you free stuff for your birthday? I've got ya covered. Bit.ly/freebirthdays Want free stuff all year round? Yeah, I found **the best** places for that, too: Bit.ly/FreeOnlineStuff and Bit.ly/FreeStuffWebsites

★★★★★ **Save money on bills**

Often the biggest drain on your wallet is your monthly bills. BillCutterz.com will try to negotiate a lower rate on your recurring bills for you. They not only know pro negotiation tactics, they know about all of the unadvertised offers too. Cost? You pay them half of the money they save you—everybody wins!

★★★★★ **Get (and give) stuff for free**

Get free items ranging from furniture to appliances at your local chapter of Freecycle.org. I've gotten a free waffle iron, school supplies, a $100 lego set, even a finger-painting set!
Another great option is **BuyNothing.**
https://BuyNothingProject.org

★★★★★ **Save money online**

- Before you buy items online, go to DealNews.com or SlickDeals.net (to search for the best current sales), RetailMeNot.com (for the newest coupon codes), then TopCashBack.com (sign in to make the purchase, and you will get a small percentage of your purchase price back). You'll save *thousands* over time. Want a more integrated solution? Install the Rakuten extension and it finds discounts *for you* while you surf.

- Also check out CamelCamelCamel.com to track prices on Amazon.com and get an email when an item you are interested in gets a price drop! A similar price-tracking service is EreaderIQ for Amazon eBooks.
- Know any gamers? Never pay full price for video games with price tracking websites or discount digital storefronts. While I can't give you specific recommendations, for most PC games just google "discount steam key" and the name of the game (make sure to look up the reputation of the site), but I haven't had a bad experience yet. For Switch games, I can specifically recommend Dekudeals.com that will alert you when a game goes on the best sale.
- Before you buy an item in a store, scan its barcode with the ShopSavvy.com app. It will show you the best price online and reviews for the product, allows you to save your products

into wish lists, and alerts you of price changes!

- Finally, before you make any big purchase you'd be doing yourself a **huge** favor by performing a quick internet search with the name or model number of the product and the word 'review'—often items are such "a good deal" because it is such poor quality that it is actually a waste of money. Take advantage of the wealth of information available to you online, and know what you're getting yourself into *before* you buy.

★★★★ Turn an old, slow computer into one that is faster than it was new!

This sounds too good to be true—and the catch is that it requires some setup—but it's legit: turn just about any computer that is less than 5 years old (though I've tried it on older… and it still worked GREAT) into a Chromebook. It's called ChromeOS Flex. Completely free (for personal use). Neverware.com

★★★ Make selling your stuff easier

To sell your old stuff in a way that doesn't rip you off as much as most trade-in offers you find advertised at local stores, yet doesn't take as much time or risk as Craigslist or selling it on eBay, check out *OfferUp (OfferUpNow.com)*. It is also a great place to buy used items—you can even set alerts on specific items. Used iPads for a fraction of retail price? Check. *A Great alternatives is Gazelle (Gazelle.com for cell phones only).*

★★★ Avoid ATM fees
Are you being charged ATM fees by your financial institution? There are ways to avoid them. Ask your bank. Some companies such as Charles Schwab or Ally bank will reimburse ATM fees you incur (visit the links for more information). I've never looked back. For a list of more banks that offer ATM reimbursements, see this article (Bit.ly/1xYwtIY).

★★ Car shopping
TrueCar.com shows you the average price people in your area are paying for the car you want. Buy from a dealer in the TrueCar network, and you can skip haggling altogether!

General tips that you probably have heard (but reminders help):
Most already know this, but consider buying clothes at thrift stores, couponing, going without cable TV (see the "Entertainment" section for many ways to do this *without* giving up your shows), getting a deep freezer (and buying sales in bulk), waiting a week to buy any large purchases that aren't absolute needs,

and paying more than the monthly minimum on your credit cards. The payoffs are *huge* over time.

Party Lifehacks

★★★ Invitations
You don't have to resort to boring emails or Facebook event pages for your parties. There are a lot of great choices for sending professional-looking invitations and keeping track of attendees with ease. I like Celebrations.com, Evite.com, PaperlessPost.com and EventBrite.com.

★★ Bowl in a bag
Want to serve bagged chips, goodies, etc. at your event, but don't have a serving bowl for them? Check out the video link Youtu.be/xPrEjcZ9GqU to instantly turn the bag **into** a "bowl." No more need to dirty up serving bowls.

★★ Chill beverages in no time
Forgot to put to put the 'cold ones' (or soda) in the fridge for enough time to make them cold? Put the bottles or cans in ice water with 2 cups of salt; they'll be cold in 3 minutes. Another option is wrapping each in a wet paper towel and putting them in the freezer for 15 minutes. Don't forget to take them out! Set a timer.

★ Keep candy from melting before it gets in your

mouth

Throwing an outdoor party with candy that melts? Put those individually-wrapped candies in a bucket with a big block of ice. Problem solved.

Privacy/Security Lifehacks

★★★★★ Finally be freed from password tracking!

LastPass.com is a cost effective, award-winning, multiplatform app that will input and remember all of your passwords with one master password. Essential.

★★★★★ Privacy management

Outside a full VPN, I recommend using protection when you go online. A free browser extension called Disconnect (Disconnect.Me) stops companies from tracking your activities online. *A* great alternative is *Ghostery.com*

Online protection, simplified.
Join over 3 million people who use our open source software to protect their identities and sensitive personal info from hackers and trackers.

Get Disconnect   Learn More   D.

★★★★ Guard your inbox from spam

Most have a secondary email account they use for less important things, but the next step is a truly temporary email address. Temp-Mail.org lets you receive email messages you don't want sent to your personal inbox, without needing to sign up and give any personal information.

★★★ Security breach notifications
HaveIBeenPwned.com lets you know if your information has been compromised in any major online security breaches. The site will even send you an alert!

★★★ Google you
Visit Google.com/ads/preferences to see how old Google thinks you are, what you are interested in, and more. Credit: Quora user Federic Haddad.

★★ Preview a site before you register
Ever been to a website that you only want to use once, but requires you to register? BugMeNot.com has a database of pre-registered usernames/passwords that anyone can use for sites requiring registration (BugMeNot.com is not kept very up to date, but I found a handful of sites that still have valid username/password accounts available for use).

★ File protection
Scan a file with 40+ antivirus engines at once at Metadefender.com or Jotti.org.

Productivity Lifehacks

Hofstadter's law: "It always takes longer than you expect, even when you take into account Hofstadter's law."

Parkinson's law – "Work expands to fill the time available for its completion." Corollary: "Expenditure rises to meet income." Coined by C. Northcote Parkinson

★ ★ ★ ★ ★ Evernote—organize your life

Evernote is the ultimate organizational tool. Evernote is available as a downloadable software program, browser extension, and app on every major platform, and it's able to store all the digital information you can think of. This magical tool has become my *personal* Google, allowing me to capture and process more than 100 times the information of a general internet user. Use Evernote for saving quotes, article excerpts, receipts (words in images are automatically turned into searchable text), project resources, recipes, and much more! If you want the *most* out of this game-changing tool, take my online course. LearnedEmpowerment.com/portfolio/tame-the-flow

★ ★ ★ ★ Task management

Though I use Evernote for all my information, my go-to app for organizing my tasks is definitely

Microsoft's multi-platform To-Do app (To-do.office.com/tasks). Take my course about organizing your time and this will CHANGE YOUR LIFE (contact me at learnedempowerment@gmail.com).

—WorkFlowy.com is another list tool that keeps track of brainstorms, to-do's, goals, etc. to an infinite degree for free (basic version). Apps also available.

★★★★ Read Text Faster

This one always trips up my mind. So, copy and paste the text into Spreeder (Spreeder.com/app.php); the site will show you the words at a much higher rate than normal. Use it to help you to speed read! ITS CRAZY how fast your brain keeps up.

★★★★ Cross-platform information sharing

Installing Pushbullet (PushBullet.com) on all your mobile devices and Chrome enables you to easily transfer information among devices and platforms (e.g., send a webpage from your phone or tablet to your desktop quicker than emailing it to yourself). With the addition of Pushbullet People, it is also an effective way to communicate with friends and family instantly.

★★★ One More Opportunity to Remember, Or Be Inspired

I didn't know until recently, but dry erase markers can be safely used on any mirror—you can use it as one more opportunity for an inspiring quote, daily reminders, or a place for a particularly pending task.

★★★ Time your tasks

Moosti.com enables you to set a countdown timer for the task you are working on (I recommend 20-minute increments). This tool really does motivate you to complete your task!

—You can also type "set timer (x) minutes" into Google for a quick timer. E.ggtimer.com is another option. For time tracking, try Toggl.com or Klok (GetKlok.com).

★★ Concentration boosting music

FocusAtWill.com claims to increase focus by playing music that scientifically optimizes brain activity. For me, the site just provides a great music selection—but it can't hurt! 30-day free trial available.

★★ Note taking and document collaboration

Notes.io is a simple note-taking website that lets you keep track of some notes, and send links to those notes to other people. *Quip.com is a similar site, with **great** collaboration features.*

Play Around with Quip

Quip isn't just your normal piece of paper. Tinker with some of the cool features in this little playground.

Shared & Interactive Task Lists

Interactive checklists make it easy to coordinate work, whether it's to plan a project, a party, or a trip.

- ☐ ← Click the box on your left to cross off the task.
- ☑ ← ~~Click again to undo it.~~

This playground document is filled with fun things to try. Check them off as you go along!

Conversations and Documents, All in One Place

No more emailing back and forth to discuss notes and changes.

- ☐ Click the yellow comment bubble on the left to join in the conversation.
- ☐ You can also comment on specific sections of text .

★★ Audio broadcasting

Want to set up an audio broadcast quickly and easily? Mixlr.com lets you easily stream audio live (think glorified conference call).

★★ Kill time-killers

Block distracting websites (*cough* Facebook) with RescueTime.com or StayFocused (browser extension).

★★   Instant polling

Speaking of presentations, PollEverywhere.com lets your audience give feedback or answer questions (multiple choice or open-ended) by sending a text message from their phones to a generated number. It's so simple, and you can also answer via the web or through Twitter (x)! The free version is limited to 25 responses.

Social/Networking Lifehacks

★★★★★ Meetup.com

Meetup.com is the ultimate resource for meeting people with shared interests or goals. Want to play board games with others? Find people to play a sport with? Explore nature? Talk about philosophy or Japanese cartoons or how to start a business? Meetup.com likely has a club about anything you want to do (if not, create your own club around just about any topic), and it allows you to expand your network to boot. I have received several job offers through contacts I met using this website. Participating in organizations that are relevant to your goals and passions offers a vital support network for your personal and professional life.

BONUS: Joining online Facebook groups around my interests (books, travel, board games, video games, parenting, technology, life hacks, etc.) has been one of THE most satisfying life decisions I've ever made. Why enjoy something only alone when you can SHARE joy WITH others (when you want)?

★★★★★ Never have to plan a date again.

If you're like me, you have people in your life. People who must be entertained. Often romantically. I wrote another book about the best date ideas that require only the smallest amount of time to plan. With ideas named things like "Face Race," "Musical Duel," and "The Noticing Game"… You should really check it out. It's called 101+ Charming Date Ideas http://amzn.to/1EbVd0B   #ShamelessSelfPromotion

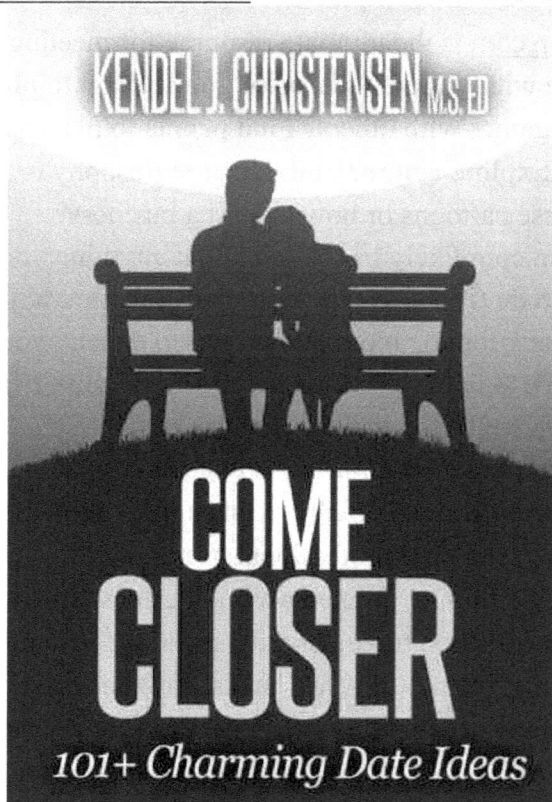

★★★★ **Watch videos "together" while apart.** Speaking of friends and dating, Teleparty (TeleParty.com) is a browser extension that lets you watch any browser-playable video with others at the same time. For example, you and a friend can watch Netflix or YouTube videos in your respective homes

without having to both try and click the play button at the same time. Hyperbeam does the same thing with some added features like shared web browsing. Watch.HyperBeam.com

★★★★★ Get gifts people *really* want

Want gift ideas for a particular person which are both personal and relevant? Type in an individual's email address on Amazon's wish list registry; if they have made their list public, you can see everything they've added to their wish list. Amazon.com/gp/registry/wishlist/search.html. Very useful!

★★★★ Video messaging

Send video emails with MailVu.com (free on the website built-in widget, $30/yr after the free, 2-week trial, or BombBomb.com. Just record yourself and the message is sent to their inbox—no downloading required. Great for a more personal way to communicate, following up with people, and saying thank you. If you want to stand out to new contacts, using these tools can be a solid "plus" in your favor.

★★★ Keep in touch with the personalization only your voice can provide

Let's face it. The digital age has affected our relationships. We text and email a lot, because it's easy. But much is lost without voice inflection and body language. The Voxer app (Voxer.com) solves half of that problem. It has the flexibility of a text message (you send a message or respond to a message when it's convenient), but with the personalization of your voice. Think "digital walkie-talkie" app for your phone. My friends and I use it to keep in touch with the understanding that a vox doesn't have the urgency of a missed call—get to it when you can. Over time, however, a series of vox messages is almost as good as a deep conversation—plus you avoid the "man, I don't keep in touch with them anymore" guilt. Highly recommend. One warning though, don't sign up with Facebook! "You will get billions of 'so and so' added Voxer! Send them a message!" alerts—which I have found no elegant way to prevent.

★★★ Keep in touch in a personal AND convenient way.

What if you could actually send PHYSICAL LETTERS (remember those?!) to people with the same convenience as sending an email? You can. Check out MailALetter.com or PostalMethods.com. They both send postal mail using the web.

★★★ Free conference calling

With FreeConferenceCall.com, up to 1000 people for up to 6 hours can make a conference call for free. The site gives you a number to dial and an access code. Useful!

★★★ Word play in texting

I am continually finding new ways to impress people with this simple trick: FlipText.org turns any message you type so that the letters are upside down. I've copied and pasted this successfully into Twitter/x, Facebook, even text messages from my phone!

★★ Call an expert

Clarity.fm connects you with people with expertise in a variety of business-related fields and industries. You pay by the minute to talk to them. If you are about to make a big decision, a few minutes from someone who knows a lot about the topic/task at hand is likely very worth it!

…

Remember that Hanlon's Razor states that we should *"Never attribute to malice that which is adequately explained by stupidity."* (Alternatively) *"Do not invoke conspiracy as explanation when ignorance and incompetence will suffice, as conspiracy implies intelligence.*" Think of this as a lifehack that helps you remain calmer when people do things that frustrate you. Works for me!

Tech/App Lifehacks

★★★★★ Enable useful services to work
together

Ifttt.com (stands for "If this, then that"). This tool allows you to connect multiple apps/accounts/services together with the statement "if ___ then ___." For example:

If [I get a Gmail attachment] then [Send it to Google drive]

If [I update my Facebook status] then [Save it to a log file in Evernote]

If [Someone tags me in a Facebook photo] then [Download the picture to Dropbox]

You can even call your phone by sending a text message to yourself (ifttt.com/applets/Yhbf3aQ7-help-me-escape) I admit as an introvert, I use this a lot to leave situations early. There are many, very powerful possibilities. Explore all the shortcuts (called Applets) I use this service extensively.

★★★★★ Phone Hacks (Pixel only)

If you own a Pixel by Google phone (my preference), you have a few unique superpowers.

First, there is a free recorder app that, more than transcribing all the words as you record... it's so fast and good that it *lets you see the conversation in real time as it happens*, Super useful for high stakes conversations where people deny what they said. (and you can save and share the recording--with the words--in the cloud.

An alternative multiplatform service is Otter.Ai.

The second I think everyone should know is a pixel

phone allows you to copy and paste any text by "swiping up" from the bottom of any screen and highlighting what you want. Sure, most websites and apps let you copy and paste natively, but many don't! As a researcher, I use this hack *multiple times per day* to cite or share something. A good workaround is using the "Lens" app (Lens.google; available on both Android and iPhone) to scan your screen and that works too to select any text.

★★★★★ LibreOffice—the "other" Microsoft Office

Did you know there's a FREE alternative to Microsoft Office? Check out LibreOffice.org—it has all the basic features of Word, Excel, and even PowerPoint. True Microsoft products are clearly better for compatibility, but newer versions of LibreOffice let you save documents as a .doc file and I've had very minimal formatting issues over the years.

BONUS: You can get an online-only version of office for free from Microsoft by visiting www.office.com and logging in.

★★★★★ Ad-free browsing

Visit AdBlockPlus.org to get rid of most of the ads on the websites you browse. The site speeds up your browsing and minimizes distractions. It's like magic.

★★★★★ Design Pro-Quality Cards and Digital Shareables

Canva.com a freemium service that I've used to make winning memes, quote posters, even party invitations and T-shirt designs (all free)--more than a full creation tool, I daresay it's a pseudo leveler between the amateur and pro designer.

Check out Infogr.am and PiktoChart.com for other ways to visualize information.

★★★★★ File recovery

Accidentally delete important pictures or documents? There are ways to resurrect your files! For Windows, check out Recuva (Piriform.com/Recuva). For Mac, try Disk Drill (CleverFiles.com). Both tools are free.

★★★★★ Explain Techy Things to Non-Tech People

Have a friend, parent, or relative that doesn't "get" technology and you don't exactly have time to sit down and explain it to them? No worries. TechBoomers.com's mission is to provide free, clear, and up-to-date lessons that teach the least tech-savvy among us how to understand and use the most popular tech services and websites.

★★★★ Free photo editors

Gimp.com is a free alternative to Photoshop. *Other great options include Pixlr (Apps.Pixlr.com/editor), GetPaint.net, and PicMonkey.com.* If you need a free video editor, look no further than AdobeExpress And Coverr.co and UnSplash.com are great collections of FREE stock images!

★★★★ Send Files Among Any Devices, Easily!

Need to send something from your phone to computer or vice versa? Simple! Connect to the same Wifi, open a browser on both devices to Snapdrop.net and click it on over. I use it constantly. Works like AirDrop, but more universal.

★★★★ Solid replacement scanner

Turn your smart phone into a scanner with CamScanner (CamScanner.com); amazing quality for a phone! Free and paid app versions available.

★★★★ Identify what is taking up space on your hard drive

Has your Windows computer run out of hard disk space? WinDirStat (WinDirStat.info) displays your *entire* hard drive in an alluringly-beautiful map to identify your biggest space hogs. I use this **all** the time.

★★★★ Product key recovery

Need to reinstall a program but can't find the product key? Magical Jelly Bean KeyFinder (MagicalJellyBean.com/KeyFinder) has saved me numerous times—it will search your computer and deliver the product key information of many of your currently installed programs. BAM! BelarcAdvisor does the same thing.

★★★★ Restore Old Photos, Free!

Got an old photo album with treasured photos that too low resolution, or even damaged? Scan them into GFP-GAN (App.baseten.co/apps/QPp4nPE/operator_views/Rqg OnqV) and watch at how they magically are restored by the power of AI. Handy!

★★★ File backups

Speaking of reinstalling things, make sure to back up your files! There are so many ways to accomplish this, from external hard drives—I use SyncBackSE (Bit.ly/14UVNUn), to online backup solutions (just do an internet search for "online backup compared"). One stand-out entry is Amazon Glacier (aws.amazon.com/glacier/). It costs pennies on the dollar; I pay just ~$.70 per month to back up the last 15 years of my digital life. The catch? You have to request the files about 4 hours in advance before they are available to download. Using this handy guide (Bit.ly/1Ccow4m) courtesy of Lifehacker, I was backing up my entire life in just 30 minutes.

UPDATE: With the advent of Google Photos (Photos.Google.com) I have almost no need for extensive backups (as most of my data is photos). Why? They will backup ALL of your photos and videos (from *all* of your devices) FOR FREE. Just make sure to upload them at "high quality" rather than "original quality."

★★★ Digital slideshows

Stupeflix.com stitches your photos and video clips together into a beautiful presentation; great for weddings, vacations, or any other memorable event.

—Other excellent video creation tools are Intro Designer for iOS (Introdesignerapp.com) or VideoScribe for Android (Bit.ly/1I5MC0k).

★★★ Easily send text messages from your computer

iPhone users can send SMS text messages from their computers, and Android can too if you use the default messaging app. But if you use any other message service, this app comes in handy and integrates with

Gmail. Mightytext.net

★★★ Video conversion
Need to convert your video into a different format?
No sweat. Visit video.online-convert.com.

★★★ Free audio editor
Edit audio clips for free using Audacity
(Audacity.sourceforge.net).

★★★ Mind mapping + Unique ways to Organize Info
MindMeister.com or Bubbl.us are free online mind
mapping tools; some of the best ways to organize
complex or interrelated ideas. I've used these sites to
help me summarize entire books, as well as answer
questions like "What is my purpose in life?" *Lately,
I've been favoring iThoughts on iPad
(Toketaware.com/iThoughts-ios) for my mind
mapping needs.* Need to just make a cute word cloud?
Wordart.com has lots of great customizable options.
And I have to mention an easy way to make timelines
online with Tiki-toki.com

★★★ Link paper files to digital versions
TagMyDoc.com enables you to add QR codes (those

funky square images you can scan with your cellphone—QR stands for "quick response") to your printed documents and presentations that link to a digital copy of the handout. Very useful for when people ask "Can you email me a digital copy of this?" Instead of me (or you) remembering to email them, they can just scan the code and get the doc themselves by using their smart phones (Free and paid versions available).

★★★ Play Android apps on your Windows or Mac
Run Android device apps on Windows and Mac machines in full screen mode with BlueStacks.com.

★★★ Create free video tutorials
Jing (techsmith.com/jing.html) empowers you to add a voice-over while recording live actions on your computer screen so you can explain a concept or process to someone quickly. I use the site to explain how to use programs or websites (there is a 5 minute limit to your video length). *Screencast-o-matic.com* and OBS are a similar free services to record your screen.

★★★ Is my phone REALLY compatible?
We've reached the day when getting the latest smartphone directly through your carrier is hardly a

good deal. A consumer now needs to get savvy finding their own deal or face getting *majorly* ripped off. This website answers the question "is my phone compatible with my network?" once and for all. www.frequencycheck.com

★★ PDF text recognition

Need to extract text from a pdf? Onlineocr.net recognizes 46 languages of text and converts the scanned pdf to a pdf with editable text.

★★ Laptop battery-saving hack

You know the brightness on your laptop? Well, what you might not know is that it's exponential. Which means the difference between setting it at 80% vs 100% is requires something like 4x as much power as the difference between 30% and 50%. Keeping that in mind has helped my battery life significantly!

★★ Online fax machine

Use FaxZero.com to send basic faxes; the free version is limited to 3 pages max, 2 faxes per day, and the site puts an ad on the cover page. GotFreeFax.com is similarly limited but (as of this writing) does not place any ads.

★★ Share large files

Send large files simply with WeTransfer.com (links are valid for 1 week) or JustBeamIt.com (near-instant transfer, but links are valid for only 10 minutes). *Other great options are SendBigFiles.com, SendThisFile.com, and Dropsend.com.*

★★ Social media scheduling

Buffer (BufferApp.com) enables you to *schedule* tweets and Facebook posts in advance, allowing you to keep up an active social media presence without actually spending too much time logged in.

★★ Super tweets

Tweet more than 140 characters with TallTweets.com; the site turns your tweet into a picture!

★★ Chatting and screen sharing

Google Hangouts (Bit.ly/1DhMY2S) is like Skype, only better (though both are constantly updating and improving). I especially like Hangouts for the ability to easily share your screen with anyone (great for troubleshooting Grandma's computer). *Join.me is a more business-friendly way to share your screen.*

★ What's that font?

Myfonts.com/whatthefont helps you determine the

name of font based on an image of text.

★ **Phone chargers and non-forgetting:**
Always buy an extra battery and chargers for your phone (and consider also: your laptop's charger). Keep them in your car. You will use them, trust me. BONUS: Always keep extras of anything you need BOTH at home and on the go. I can't tell you how much time I've saved knowing there was already scissors or a battery pack *already* in my car. One less thing to have to think about!
DOUBLE BONUS: Put an emergency $20 in your phone (in between the phone and its case). It DEFINITELY comes in handy! Think of all the times you've been frustrated at cash-only place or forgotten your wallet.

Time-saving Lifehacks

★★★★★ Get Things DONE

Of all the methods I go over clients with, David Allen's Getting Things Done method has helped the most. Watch his TED talk, then follow my summary below. Create a system that you TRUST that:
1. CAPTURES the important thing
2. Makes it CLEAR & ACTIONABLE
3. "Parks" the information so its where and when YOU need it
4. Follow up on your PRIORITIES
Remember: you can't do EVERYTHING that is important, accept that as NORMAL.

Contact me for one on one efficiency and time management coaching!

★★★★★ Saving Seconds Adds Up: Use Assistance (Assistants)!

There are lots of ways to accomplish tasks. But to save time, I strongly encourage you to install ways in your life to do the tasks the most efficient way possible. Acknowledging legitimate privacy concerns, I still think smart displays and speakers (e.g., Alexa, Google Home/Nest, Apple Homepod) in your home is a huge win for this. The entry-level speakers are routinely $10 in your local marketplace listings/classifieds. For example,

- Never have to get up to turn off the lights

again (install a smart light switch, and you turn all the main lights on and off with your voice! Or at least an app)

- You can ask them to "Find my phone" in seconds (I've used this *dozens* of times)
- Entertain kids with jokes and stories and videos (smart displays only)
- Make calls and check things like when an establishment closes (I always forget when my local UPS store and library closes lol)
- Get news updates or listen to an audiobook while you're in the bathroom
- Broadcast announcements to your whole household, etc. The possibilities are so vast!

★★★★★ Don't Forget as Often

After hundreds of hours researching memory techniques (let me know on www.learnedempowerment.com if you want a dedicate course), and one of the simplest—yeah, I know its simple, but it really works—is remembering to remember. Take an extra few seconds to do any action you want to remember more "consciously" like where you put your keys or wallet (remember: our brains evolved in an era where *all we had* was the present moment—no ability write, save, or do anything except tell stories and rely on our memory!):

1. When putting them away, Say it to yourself aloud e.g., "Keys on counter", "Wallet in left drawer" and

2. Be mindful as you are performing the action– Consciously watch your hand put the wallet in the drawer when you utter "Wallet in left drawer". That 'moment' is now embedded in your brain as a more important memory so that when "keys" or "wallet" comes to your mind again, that moment will be associated with it. If you spend time to make this a habit, the question "Where is my wallet?" will automatically bring to mind where you left it.

3. Related to general memory tips: making up or telling a *story* about it, increases retention manifold. The best tip here is to make the story as *vivid* as possible. Think about it: when you're neighbor did something CRAZY, it sticks in your mind! Leverage that!

—A related tip is to place 'other' important items next to your wallet or keys so you don't forget to bring them along.

BONUS memory tip: Remember everything better from lists to speeches with the "memory palace" technique:

www.YouTube.com/watch?v=dMIx8pzYBlo

DOUBLE BONUS: Want the most consistent best way to remember something? Teach it to someone else. Seriously, which of your friends would say 'no' to you calling them up and saying "I just learned this thing and HAD to tell you about it!" Win-win!

★★★★★ Hired help

Need something done? Try FancyHands.com, Fiverr.com, UpWork.com, or TaskRabbit.com. These services outsource some tasks you can't or don't want to do for a small fee. Your life will never be the same again. Most tasks are limited to things that your hired help doesn't have to be *physically* present for (taskrabbit is the exception). *Of note, Zirtual.com is significantly more expensive, but, like Fancyhands, relies on employees in the USA.*

★★★★★ Pick a meeting time

When2Meet.com helps you stop emailing back and for the find the best time for everyone to meet. When2Meet makes finding an ideal time for an event/meeting a breeze—no registration required! The site stacks each person's "available time" on top of each other. The darkest area is the time that works for the most people.

Group's Availability

0/5 Available ▭▭▭▭▭ 5/5 Available

Mouseover the Calendar to See Who Is Available

	Mon	Tue	Wed	Thu	Fri	Sat
9 AM						
10 AM						
11 AM						
Noon						
1 PM						
2 PM						
3 PM						
4 PM						
5 PM						
6 PM						
7 PM						
8 PM						
9 PM						
10 PM						

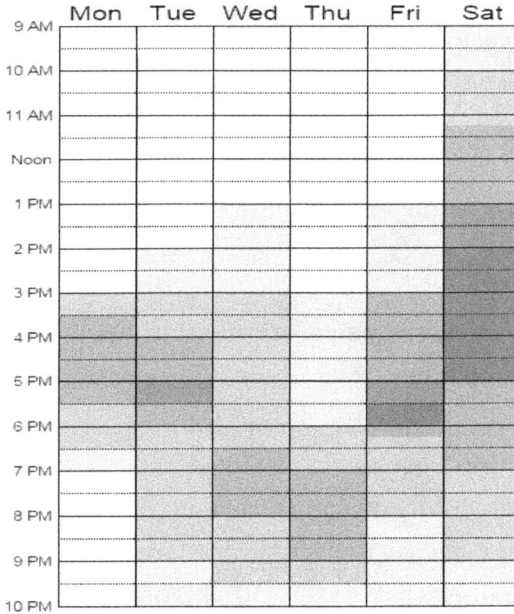

*A popular alternative for these same features is
<u>Doodle.com.</u> With <u>YouCanBook.me</u> people can sign
up for "available spots" in your calendar.
<u>WhichDateWorks.com</u> has been mentioned as a good
alternative as well.*

★★★★★ Have someone do the "which product is best" research for you

I wish I would have known about this site sooner:

TheWirecutter.com. This site regularly compares a wide variety of items for you (including Appliances, electronics, even pillows and razors), and recommends only the best. Unlike most "best of" experts, I actually agree with their conclusions when I do my own analysis. Their buying guides usefully divide up their best picks by: Best overall for most people, best value pick, and best "upgrade" pick. Handy!

★★★ Sites and service recommendations

Find the best computer program or service in any category through AlternativeTo.net or SimilarSites.com. I use this *constantly.* When a friend tells me about a cool new app or website, I type it into alternativeto.net in case there's another website that does the same thing that is rated 50x higher!

★★★★ Press the magic button to reach a customer representative

GetHuman.com tells you how to navigate through those annoying pre-recorded phone menus and straight to a real customer service representative. The site also lists direct numbers for companies as well as offers a feature where the companies call *you.*

★★★★ House hunting

Moving? Find the ideal place to live by filtering options from meta-housing-search service PadMapper.com.

★ ★ ★ ★ Clipboard manager

Save hours every week by using a clipboard manager program that automatically keeps track of the things you've previously copied and pasted. I recommend ArsClip, Ditto, or PhraseExpress.

★ ★ ★ Bite-sized news

The Skimm (theSkimm.com). Don't have time to keep up on the national news? The Skimm delivers to your inbox the most popular articles reduced down to bite-sized summaries written in layman's terms. *Vox.com is similarly written in a very accessible way, but is intended for people looking for a fuller background to any given story.*

★ ★ ★ Copy text from images

Want to quickly extract the text from an image? Paste the text into Microsoft OneNote (free), then right-click on the image and select "copy text from picture." Evernote is also free and has a similar feature—right click and select "paste as text." Plus, the text in all images saved in Evernote is automatically searchable.

★★ Keyboard Shortcuts

If you accidentally close a tab, **Ctrl + Shift + t** (**Command-Shift-T** on Mac) reopens it.

If you want to change text to make it ALL CAPS (or turn all caps into lower-case), hold down Shift + F3 (add + fn if you're using a Mac).

★★ Free dictation

If your computer has a microphone, go to Dictation.io for free dictation. Talking at my computer and having it type everything I say never gets old! If you already have a recording and need to transcribe it, oTranscribe.com makes that task significantly less painful.

★ Random generators

With Random.org you can pick random numbers, flip a virtual coin, and other unbiased random generators.

Travel Lifehacks

★★★★★ Travel hacking

Want to travel the world for cheap, or even practically free? Embrace "travel-hacking" (note: applying for credit cards required). Get started by visiting Bit.ly/1qI0ER6, or Google the phrase. There is a veritable trove of great information out there. Using these tips (and some old-fashioned luck), I've gotten about $12,000 worth of flights for about $550 over the past 12 years.

★★★★★ Free insider travel advice

Never go to a terrible restaurant or hotel again. Before you go to a place to eat, check Yelp.com (apps also available). Before you check out an attraction or hotel, check TripAdvisor.com (apps available). They have a large selection of user ratings and tips that can make all the difference in how your plans turn out, including the best pre-made lists of attractions to any city.

★★★★ Next-Level Travel Planning

When I plan a trip, it's a mess of Google Docs, emails, and an excel sheet with museum hours. All of that is eliminated with Wanderlog.com, an app that is your new second brain when it comes to trip organizing. Top features are keeping track of all venue hours, an ability to make a SIMPLE day to day itinerary (with the ability to quickly re-order any plans by dragging and dropping) and travel estimates between places. Let the company themselves explain all the other many features including itinerary sharing at youtu.be/HFWgThplaLw

—Roadtrippers.com also shares places of interest near your destination. Apps also available.

★★★★ Translation

Google Translate (Translate.Google.com – apps also available) isn't perfect, but it gets more amazing by the day. Simply talk to the app, and Google Translate will spit out not only what you wrote and its written translation, but pronounce the translation for you as well. Currently, the app supports translation in 90 different languages. Google recently added a feature where you can point your smartphone camera at words (e.g., a sign), and the app will translate the words for you *in real time.*

★★★ Get rides cheaper than taxis.

The Uber and Lyft apps are excellent (and usually *much* cheaper) alternatives to taking a regular taxi. Using GPS in your phone, they come to where you are!

★★★ Free and cheap accommodations

CouchSurfing.com offers free accommodations (but don't expect higher quality than a spare couch). Also, be *very* careful in choosing who to trust—check the user ratings before committing. *Another great accommodations service that will save you gobs of money over hotels is AirBnB.com.* Accommodations vary (from the spare room in an apartment to a full house).

—To save money on last-minute hotel reservations, the HotelTonight.com app can offer incredible savings.

—Traveling and need someone to take care of a pet? Dog Vacay (DogVacay.com) has you covered. About $40 per night.

★★ Virtual Mailman

Going out of town but still want to read your mail? VirtualPostMail.com will scan your mail so you can view it online as it arrives—ideal for traveling. From the site: "The unopened envelopes are scanned so you can see your mail online. You then decide whether to have the mail opened and scanned, forwarded, or trashed." Pricing from $5–$30 per month.

★★ Value Flight Finder

Skyscanner.com is a flight search engine with a twist: the site tells you the cheapest flights out of your airport. Very useful if you want to travel but don't know where.

★★ Hands Free Entertainment

Though many flights offer plenty of in-flight entertainment, I'm surprised at how often I'm on my own on a long flight. This hack has come in handy more than a handful of times.

Credit: claireadelie

Wellness Lifehacks

★★★★★ Small Happiness Hack

It sounds simple, but according to research at Yale, this one habit can make a BIG difference in your daily happiness: Take 15 seconds every day (I do it before my first bite of breakfast—see the "anchor habit" hack for fitness) and think:

Of something you have in your life: something you like or enjoy.

Then imagine your life if that thing did not exist.

Then remember, that you do, in fact, have it.

That's it!

BONUS: The founder of LinkedIn says the habit that makes the most difference in his day is to write a "nice note" to someone in your life (I do "nice texts"). I testify there is almost *nothing* that makes another person's day as to be thought of and remembered and given positive attention. The hack, though, is the fact that when *you* make someone's day, *you tend to feel really **great.*** I know this to be true.

DOUBLE BONUS: Write a personal gratitude message this for someone—a friend that you've not seen in awhile or not kept up with, an acquaintance you want to become a friend—, and just add that you want to catch up: a call, video chat, or go out to lunch. After just a few months you'll have a whole new supportive social group. HUGE difference in the happiness for most people (definitely for me!).

★★★★★ Life-changing Happiness Hack

Yet another theme building from the last hack, the longtime head of the APA, Martin Seligman recommends, as one of the absolute highlights of a person's life, to write a longer praising letter to someone you care about. Print it out. Go to their house. Ring the doorbell. Ask if you can read it to them. Then give it to them. His research indicates that it will not soon be forgotten for anyone involved. Hard to do (especially for me as an introvert!) but the research is clear: Life. Changing.

★★★★★ Small hack to feel better towards our fellow men and women:

How you think has a big effect on your happiness. Most people walk around thinking that the things that happen to them and the things people do that they don't like are because the person is deliberately trying to harm them. Instead, adopt Hanlon's razor **"Don't attribute to malice, what can adequately be explained by ignorance"** Or, better yet, adopt Dr. Dan Ariely's method of thinking about others' actions after doing a lifetime of research on human nature:

[Combine] "Never attribute to malice that which can be adequately explained by human fallibility," and Occam's razor, "The simplest explanation is the one we should favor, until it is proven to be inadequate." To these we can add Hitchens' razor…: "What can be asserted without evidence can also be dismissed without evidence." Together, these three tools can prevent us from falling into a spiral of misbelief.

They invite us to ask questions such as: **Is it reasonable to assume malicious intent over**

stupidity, human fallibility, or chance? Is it sensible to propose a complex web of ill intention? Do I have the necessary evidence to support such an extraordinary claim? If the things we're trying to explain don't pass the test of these three razors, it's a sign that we should take a step back and suspect that we're onto the wrong explanation. We can also use these three razors in conversations with others to challenge their biases toward intentionality, complexity, and insufficient evidence." (*Misbelief*, page 95, 2023 Harper Collins, New York)

--How much better would the world be if we followed this rather than making so many ASSumptions?--

Health & Beauty

★★★★★ Free answers to health questions

I have to say I am impressed with HealthTap.com's mission to create "the world's most trusted online health companion." Here's how it works: you pose a question and *real* physicians answer them. For free. They are adding features all the time (like listing and rating local doctors). For a private video consultation, it is $9.99 per question (with a free follow-up question). Apps available.

★★★ Cultivate a healthy mood

Calm.com plays calming music and soothing visuals for free. *Noisli.com is similar, and has been touted as being helpful in increasing productivity and concentration.*

★★ Moisturizing makeup remover

Moisturize your skin and remove makeup all in one action by applying Cold Cream (See Bit.ly/1MoLBVj).

Fitness

★★★★★ 7-Minute Workout

Want to get the best exercise in the least time? Use the now-famous "7-minute Workout" (Nyti.ms/1wnky93)—basically, do each of the exercises below for 30 seconds with a 10-second break in between. Consult a health professional before attempting. Article credit to Gretchen Reynolds, photo credit to Ben Wiseman. See also 7-min.com/help

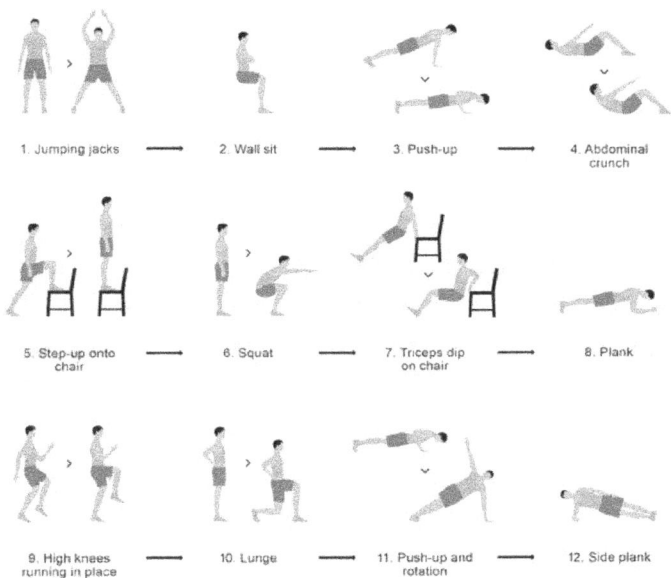

1. Jumping jacks ⟶ 2. Wall sit ⟶ 3. Push-up ⟶ 4. Abdominal crunch

5. Step-up onto chair ⟶ 6. Squat ⟶ 7. Triceps dip on chair ⟶ 8. Plank

9. High knees running in place ⟶ 10. Lunge ⟶ 11. Push-up and rotation ⟶ 12. Side plank

★★★ Keep the habit

Stickk.com makes it highly incentivizing to stick to your goals—you put money on the line. Earn money by following through on your goals (by taking the money of those who don't). *Other great creating-better-habit apps to check out are Habitica.com, Fitocracy.com, and BeeMinder.com.*

BONUS: Chip and Dan Heath in their book *Switch: How to Change When Change is Hard* recommends as one of the best habit-keeping hacks is to "anchor" the new habit to something you *already* do consistently (like brush your teeth, or do your favorite wind-down activity). Simply DON'T do the thing you always do UNTIL you've done the new thing! For me, it has created a bunch of new habits in my life! **DOUBLE BONUS**: In the landmark book, *Tiny Habits,* Author B.J. Fogg recommends a counter-intuitive approach to making habits: start *insultingly* small. If you don't floss, just say to yourself "today, I'm only going to floss one tooth"; For a running habit, put your running shoes by the door and start with *just one block.* It sounds silly, but the hack is that *once you begin anything,* **your brain is much less resistant to continuing it.** I.e., "oh, might as well floss more teeth" and before you know it, you're done and you'll form a habit. TRY IT!

★ Stay full while eating less

Want to eat less? Try putting the healthiest food at eye level in your fridge, drink two glasses of water before meals (fills your stomach and reduces appetite), and eat in front of a mirror. Note: these will, at best, result in only incremental differences, but every little bit helps.

Sleep

★★★★★ Finally! Fight the heat at night

with—literally—the coolest pillow!
I don't know about you, but at night, I often get *uncomfortably hot.* What are your options? Hopefully you can open a window or dial down the AC… but sometimes there just aren't many effective options. Enter something that has *changed my life.* It's called the Gel'O pillow mat. It's soft and *extremely* pleasant to the touch because of its ability to maintain a refreshing coolness while you fall asleep.
BONUS: Tied for most life-changing sleep accessory is my trusty Bed Jet. It cools or warms *under the sheets* at night.

★★★ Musical sleep aid
This music is scientifically designed to put you to sleep: Youtube.com/watch?v=UXgqDlrqmzo. As mentioned above, Calm.com plays calming music and soothing visuals for free. *Noisli.com is similar, and lets you create your own noise-combinations.*

★★★ Fight back against sleep deprivation.
Using a computer, tablet, or phone at night hurts the quality of your sleep by dampening your body's production of melatonin. Install F.lux (JustGetFlux.com) to reduce sleep-inhibiting blue light at night on your devices. *Twilight (Bit.ly/1GlKe5N) is a great alternative for android phones.*

Misc/Important Info to Know

Important Numbers to Know (USA)

- **Suicide Hotline** Call, text, <u>988</u> Available 24/7.
  - **Text**: Also, text "HELLO" to 741741
  - **Chat**: Visit 988lifeline.org
- **Trans Lifeline**: A peer support hotline run by trans people for trans and questioning individuals.
  - **Phone**: (877) 565-8860
  - **Text**: Text "PRIDE" to 741741 (for LGBTQ+ support)
  - **Hours**: Monday to Friday, 10 AM – 6 PM Pacific Time
- **National Domestic Violence Hotline**: For those experiencing domestic violence.
  - **Phone**: 1-800-799-7233 (SAFE)
  - **Text**: Text "START" to 88788
- **National Sexual Assault Hotline**
- **RAINN (Rape, Abuse & Incest National Network)**: For survivors of sexual violence.
  - **Phone**: 1-800-656-4673 (HOPE)
  - **Chat**: Visit RAINN.org
- **Veterans Crisis Line**: For veterans and their

loved ones.

- o **Phone**: 988 and press 1
- o **Text**: Text 838255
- o **Chat**: Visit VeteransCrisisLine.net

Thanks for Reading!

Thanks again for reading. If you enjoyed this book, please post a short review at http://amzn.to/1tYRP9k (even a few words helps!) and share this book with someone you know. I'm a self-run organization and rely on my readers for the exposure I need to succeed.

About the Author

Kendel Christensen is the founder of Learned Empowerment (www.LearnedEmpowerment.com), a Washington D.C.-based company that helps individuals become confident, capable, and in control of their lives. As an educator, speaker, and writer, Kendel is known for his unbounded enthusiasm for uncovering and conveying life-changing truths in hyper-real ways. From living in the Middle East to teaching in an inner-city high school, Kendel distills the best wisdom from experiencing the full range of life's possibilities. Kendel earned a Masters of Education from the University of Pennsylvania and a B.S. in Sociology from Brigham Young University. Ask him about his progress on memorizing 100 books, growing his personal database of 15,000+ inspiring quotes, or achieving his 140 life goals.

Thanks to:

Mrs. Caitlin Christensen, Lisa Lowe, Janet Christensen, Eric Gifford, Casey Gleave, Tyler Lefevor, Bradley Mecham, Tom Arnold, Dustin Nay, Victor Salcedo, Devin Belliston, Bryan Monson, Andrew Proctor, Christopher Cole, Emilee Thomas, Thomas Alvord, Daniel Derricott, Michael Rose, JD Itri, Jensen Vessels, Simmandi Lawrence, and Douglass Gillette.

Link to leave a review http://amzn.to/1tYRP9k (Every review, however small, helps a lot!)

---END---

www.ingramcontent.com/pod-product-compliance
Lightning Source LLC
Chambersburg PA
CBHW060511280326
41933CB00014B/2922